ENDOR⸢

CH00651751

Such an incisive play that tou⸢
of society's most detestable challenges of our time. Ola-Kris
weaves reality into an intensely emotional rendition of blatant
violation of human rights. Although set in the 1960s, *Ghost
Twerkers* is a hard-hitting social commentary on contemporary
gender-based atrocities that renders it simply timeless!

Prof. Rachael Diang'a, PhD
*Assistant Professor of Film and Chair of Cinematic Arts Dept.,
United States International University-Africa, Nairobi, Kenya.*

Ola-Kris, feminist scholar, artist, and a queer theorist, has
presented to us a stunningly thought-provoking play as he
reveals the dangers and silence around gender-based
violence. I had the honour of collaborating with him by
bringing my Gender Studies students to critically engage with
this intersectional play, which portrays how class, race, and
gender intersect to oppress and marginalize women. The best
way to end violence against women and girls is to prevent it
from happening in the first place by addressing its root and
structural causes, such as patriarchy. Twenty-six years into
democracy, South Africa is still grappling with gender
inequality and gender-based violence. The play impacts and
probes scholars and activists to continue the conversations on
rape, femicide, gender-based violence, patriarchy, inequality,
and the justice system. We must stop asking victims 'what
were you wearing' and reemphasise that 'real men do not
rape', 'real men do not kill'.

Mrs Samukezi Mrubula-Ngwenya
Dept. of Cultural and Political Studies, University of Limpopo.

From the very first scene, one immediately got a sense that the
play was a realistic depiction of how deep gender-based
violence is in South Africa and how the justice system is not

often the immediate option for victims. It also showed that the justice system could [and should], in fact, ensure justice is served. The scene of a younger brother, Madala, forcing his elderly sister into forced intercourse was one of the most painful scenes, and remains etched in my memory from back in 2019 when I saw *Ghost Twerkers'* premier.

Rebecca Phala
News Editor, Energy FM, South Africa

At no auspicious time since the independence of the Republic of South Africa has there been so much upbeat activity and concerns about Gender Based Violence (GBV) as we have witnessed within the last few years in the country and in our world. This cannot be removed from the fact that the cases of rape assaults have risen meteorically in almost every corner of our global village, with the attendant negative impact on the female population. *Ghost Twerkers*, a new play by Ola-Kris Akinola is, therefore, a thoughtful, compassionate, and delicate intervention, inspired by the irresistible urge of the playwright to give his own view of the insanity.

Ghost Twerkers renews the possibility of Hope for Justice, Dialogue, Diagnosis and Direction out of this epidemic. I have no doubt that it will penetrate the heart of judges to do justice, law enforcement agents, and medical care givers to deliver on their mandate, with a view to ameliorating this atrocity against our women and our daughters. The reader and the audience will find solace in the ritual of communion which Drama and Theatre are.

Prof. Adediran K. ADEMIJU-BEPO, PhD
Professor of Theatre and Film Studies, University of Jos, Nigeria

GHOST TWERKERS

Ola-Kris Akinola

Ghost Twerkers
Copyright © 2022 by Ola-Kris Akinola

Published by
163 Warbank Crescent,
Croydon
CR0 0AZ

ISBN: 978-1-905669-69-1

Names of places and persons in these plays are entirely fictitious. Resemblance to real names is coincidental and artistic.

Request for performance rights to be directed to:
A. The Publisher
B. Dr. O.C. Akinola
The Performing Arts Centre
University of Limpopo
South Africa

Cover concept inspired by Keren Akinola
Cover designed by Icon Media
Printed in the United Kingdom

*To the University of Limpopo community, led by
the V.C., Prof M. Mokgalong, DVCs., Prof R.
Madadzhe and Prof J. Singh, for always delighted
to watch the performances.*

*To abused women (and men) all over the world, as
well as the men (and women) who continue to add
needed balms to the emotional, psychological, and
physical wounds of the abused.*

*To the 2019 Premiere cast and crew who were my
acting students between 2015 and 2019, especially
the MALISAS who, as actresses, literally put their
bodies "on the line" of the stage, so as to depict the
graphic nature of GBV.*

AUTHOR'S PREFACE

This play is a response to the increase in rape and femicide cases in South Africa witnessed around 2018. It creates an opportunity to scale up awareness, education, including information on gender-based violence. It is my hope that the work would initiate dialogues on the scourge in order to interrogate and, perhaps, stem this evil in our world. This responsibility is owed by all of humanity, for all of humanity.

Ola-Kris Akinola

Cast & Crew for
"Ghost Twerkers" 2019 Premiere

"Ghost Twerkers" was premiered between 1-14 April, 2019 at the New Cinema Hall of the University of Limpopo, South Africa.

MALISA: Mashoto Mphahlele; Victoria Giba; Nomfundo Ndlazi; Tshego Khumalo; Refilwe Themba.

NANDY: Kopano Kgasago; Maria Mashaphu; Riiah Mashaphu.

NELLY: Mapule Mpetu; Eunice Soeka; Koketxo Sekhula; Palesa Modipane.

MEN (Rapists): Califonia Ngwepe; Silence Shokane; Chris Rabore; Jabulane Lebese.

SERGEANT MALINGO: Makungu Mbete; Gift Makola; Lesedi

GOGO: Phumelele Mabuza; Caroline Kgobe; Mbalenhle Mabasa; Precious;

MADALA: Advice Mbuyane; Kgatla Masie Foster; Chris Rabore;

DOCTOR: Lifted Olusola; Koketso Mohlapi; Relebogile Mashao.

DLAMINI: Shirley Talane; Lesego Seopane; Paul Masia; Harry Motsuki; Mokgomotsi Seshoka.

DIKKO: Unique Mashokoa; Thlologelo Masemola; Bokgomotse; Martin Ramagoshi; Mpho.

JUDGE: Countries Machate; Performance Rakgwatla; Unique Mashokoa.

COURT POLICE: Mokoka; Bonnie Mamakoko;

SERGEANT BETHRAND: Smanga Khoza; Monyela Prince;

REPORTER: Nomsa Sekgota; Favour Alawode; Neo Mokoena; Getrude Masia;

COURT TWERKER: Tumelo Shaka; Lifted Olusola;

COURT CLERK: Caroline Makhubedu

CREW
DIRECTOR: Ola-Kris Akinola.

ASS DIRECTORS: Relebogile Mashao; Unique Mashokoa.

SENIOR STAGE MANAGER: Mmabatho Maboya

TECHNICAL MANAGER: Blessing Shongwe; Lindelani Phetla.

MAKEUP MANAGER: Mashoto Mphahlele.

COSTUME MANAGER: Kopano Kgasago; Shirley Talane;

PROPS MANAGER: Mapule Mpetu.

SOUND MANAGER: Nelson Lechelele

MOVEMENT ONE

This play is set in a winter of the late 60s with costumes, props, hairstyles and make-ups presenting the 60s vintage. Gogo's tin-house, popularly called a shack, is on the far left corner of the stage and on the far right sits the police station. The court is positioned far deep on the centre stage, while the night club sits between the Court and the Police station. The Doctor's office is between the Court and Gogo's shack. Two Police officers at the station, Sergeant Malingo and detective Bethrand listen to the news on radio. Madala also listens to his hand-held radio while Gogo moves in and out of the shack. Presently, a television broadcast is projected on the screen as the reporter reports.

News Report

And here is the news in full. Violent crime in South Africa has become rife and horrific, with the escalated prevalence of sexual assault and rape leading to South Africa being labelled the rape capital of the world. This is largely attributed to the pervasive rape culture that exists in the country. Unfortunately, the criminal justice system is failing survivors as few cases are reported, with only few victims receiving justice. The nagging question is, do the civil courts offer an appropriate alternative? What we do know at the moment is that the law is simply not doing enough for rape survivors. According to the 2016/2017 crime statistics, over 100 people are raped every day in our country, and that is just based on the attacks that are reported. This means that the number of people being brutally violated adds up to tens of thousands every year.

This is Patricia Baloyi,

Southern Agency Television

MOVEMENT TWO

Night Club. Music. Gamblers. Dancers. Pot Smokers. Brawlers. Bouncers. The scene opens with a number of girls seductively twerking, pole and lap dancing for male clients who shower them with tips. Malisa, Nandi and Nelly are part of the dancers.

LIGHTS OUT

MOVEMENT THREE

It is a very cold early morning. Malisa, Nandi and Nelly from the night club stroll onto a dimly lit and quiet street, sharing a joint, laughing and showing off their twerking skills and the money they made for the night, while they wait for taxi.

ALL THE GIRLS: (Sing)
>Wont you help to sing
>These songs of freedom?
>'Cause all I ever have
>Redemption song
>Redemption song
>Redemption song
>Emancipate yourselves from
>mental slavery.
>None but ourselves can
>free our minds.

The girls laugh and exchange "Hi Fives".

NANDY: My clients tonight were
           fabulous.
           Huge tips, my friends.

NELLY: I tell you. I got good tips too,
           but some tried to be naughty,
           though. Typical of men, I must
           add.

ALL GIRLS: Typical!

All the girls laugh and exchange "Hi Fives".

MALISA: Did you see that one?

NANDY: Which one?

MALISA: The one with the jacket. He had so
            much fun when I twerked *(she
            twerks)*, but he killed the fun that
            moment he became too ambitious
            for my taste.

NANDY: Ambitious and curious.

MALITA: Exactly, too curious.

NELLY: Even rude! Like the one I danced
            for. I was dancing on his laps, fair
            enough. Then he curved his
            hands around my waist. And,
            huh! I felt a hard rock somewhere
            in between his legs. I slowly tried
            to dance away but the silly guy
            wanted more. These men always
            want more. I wonder why.

MALISA: We do our job satisfactorily.
            That is why, my friend.

NANDY: They are hungry lions. They
            want meat. That is why.

The girls laugh heartily

MALISA: Correct, Nandy. Listen mates,
            imagine the effrontery. He
            started to touch my ass as I
            twerked. This special asset. He
            touched me. Only my girlfriend
            does that.

NANDY: The idiot! But there are rules. "Do
            not touch the dancer". It is
            written boldly, in Afrikaans.

NELLY: The language of the oppressor.
            Our men hate Afrikaans as a
            language.

MALISA: Indeed. Who will admire visitors
            who subverted our lives, im-
            posing themselves, their ways
            and their language on us?

NANDY: Nonsense!

NELLY: Such disrespect! I loathe it.

MALISA: Even me. You all know that I
            have a chronic disdain for
            disrespect. I cannot deal.

NELLY: So, what did you do?

NANDY: *(playing mother)* What did you do
              child? I did not raise you to
              meddle with unproductive
              pranksters.

The girls laugh hysterically

MALISA: *(Playing child)* You know your
              girl, Mother. I said to him nicely,
              "this is strictly business brother!"

NELLY: *(Playing mother)* That is my girl.
              And then?

MALISA: *(Playing child)* Wait for it, Mama.
              And then, I tried to move his
              hand away. At first, very nicely.

NELLY: Nicely? Bad move.

NANDY: *(Playing mother)* You ought to
              have kicked his dick, and used
              the pepper spray I gave you,
              child.

NELLY: He will not stop at that. Or did he?

MALISA: And then, when the idiot would
              not flinch, I yanked the filthy
              hand away from my ass.

NELLY: Such disrespect. Who does he think he is?

NANDY: Goats. They think girls who go to night clubs are prostitutes or junkies. Some of us just want to have a good time.

NELLY: And, like us, some are just there to make a decent living. To survive. Nothing more.

ALL GIRLS: *(Near tears)* We are responsible University students.

NANDY: Men should get a life and stop treating us like we are trash.

NELLY: We want to have a good life, better than our hard working mothers and fathers. Not these abuses.

MALISA: Wait for the most disgusting part. He said to me…*(sobs)*.

NELLY: He still had the guts to speak. Brothers will never learn their lessons quietly.

NANDY: What did he say?

14

MALISA: He said to me "I am dreaming
            that I am fucking you right
            now."

NANDY
AND NELLY: What?

NANDY: The brother said that?

NELLY: He did?

MALISA: That trash of a brother said that to
            my face. Do I look like a sex doll?

NANDY: What did you tell him in
            response?

NELLY: Wait a minute. Do not tell me you
            played the dumb. I will beat your
            ass right now, child.

NANDY: What did you tell him in reply?

MALISA: Very gently and slowly, I said
            "wake up from your dream and
            go fuck your mama."

NELLY: You lie!

NANDY: You said that?

MALISA: I said it. You should have seen
            the expression on his face.

15

Priceless. As if he saw a ghost. I am no prostitute.

NELLY: We merely do this for the money.

NANDY: Nothing more. That is why we work hard.

The girls sing and dance to Donna Summer's "She Works Hard for the Money". Malisa starts to sob, Nelly and Nandy join in.

MALISA: We only want to survive. To fund our education.

NANDY: Varsity life is tough for black students. My mother is a single parent. A cleaner. Besides paying for my tuition, I fend for the family, sometimes.

NELLY: I owe heavily in school fees and I am responsible for my little brother in grade four. I just want the money, not to be objectified.

NANDY: My family, seven of us, depend on my Varsity bursary. We do this just for the money. Nothing more.

NELLY: It is business. No strings should
           be attached.

The girls cluster and sob some more. Presently, one man appears on the scene, stalking them, then a second man, a third, a fourth. a fifth and a sixth man. The girls are scared and begin to back off as the men come closer. The men catch up with them, two men on each girl, and rip their clothes as they are further beaten and then raped. The men finish the attack and leave the stage, while the girls crawl towards one another to find solace in their collective pain and grief, sobbing.

LIGHTS OUT

Rape Scene

After the rape

MOVEMENT FOUR

*Gogo is with her younger brother, Madala, a disabled
drunk. Madala is half drunk. Ongoing discussion.*

MADALA: Gogo, there is no more milk.

GOGO: Who needs milk?

MADALA: I need milk Gogo. To quench this
           babalas.

GOGO: Your liver is wasting away. Stop
           drinking.

MADALA: Is that an advice or a suggestion?

GOGO: Call it both, I care less.

MADALA: Of course, of a truth, you do not
           care. I suspected it would come
           out some day, and now it has.
           You do not care about this
           family. We always get to this
           moment. The moment when I
           always wish that I was born
           before you. I would have been a
           responsible family head.

GOGO: Indeed it is you who is the misfit
           here. Where is your ego? This

one misrepresents chauvinists. First males everywhere assume the role of family heads.

MADALA: Males everywhere?

GOGO: Responsible males, that is. Some could even be third born or last born. You will find them, everywhere.

MADALA: Exactly! Everywhere. Is this family everywhere? Take a deep breath, woman. Your grandchild goes everywhere, dancing and prostituting herself for money. Tell me, is that what decent girls everywhere do?

GOGO: Look at you. A disgrace to this family. No skill, no job, no wife, no child, no life. A useless liability. You abandoned the job at the mines. A criminal offence. Now, you hide for fear of getting arrested. You waste the air you breathe. You disgust me.

As if Gogo's last statements cleared his drunkenness. He looks at Gogo with sorrow and disbelief in his eyes.

MADALA: Now you mock me because of
            this disability. You mock your
            own brother. As usual, you will
            now be punished.

*Madala brings out a pocket knife, brandishes it at
Gogo, and then moves on her. Gogo is scared and
shows anger and helpless disdain because the abuse
has become a normal occurrence. She pleads.*

GOGO: Please!

MADALA: Too late. I warned you that you
            will be punished whenever you
            insult my masculinity or disability.
            At least I am useful for something.
            As the first male, I own this house
            built by our father. Leave if you
            are not satisfied with the way I
            treat you. Without me you cannot
            even have security. Now, put off
            your clothes.

*Gogo starts to remove clothes while Madala watches.
He begins to remove his trousers.*

LIGHTS OUT

Gogo & Madala

MOVEMENT FIVE

Police station. Malisa sits, totally unresponsive and indifferent.

SERGEANT MALINGO:

> How many were the men? Ok I remember your statement reads six *(He writes)* Six men involved in crime. Six men.

SERGEANT MALINGO:

> You said that you were three that were attacked.

MALISA: *(Looks at him viciously and nods.)*

SERGEANT MALINGO:

> Oh, sorry. Raped. You were three that were raped. I see. Three girls, women, raped. So, tell me again, you said they tied your hands, right? (He writes) Hands were tired. And only you came to the station to report? Unbelievable. Where are the other girls? Maybe only you did not enjoy it. Hahaha! Alright, I

get it. So, does it happen all the time, that only one victim out of many, in this case, three, would go to the Police station and report an offence allegedly committed against many?

Malisa does not respond.

SERGEANT MALINGO:

Okay. *(He writes)* Hands were tied. With what?

(Malisa is silent).

SERGEANT MALINGO:

Victim is irresponsive. And then, after that, they took turns in raping you all? *(Mocks)* Hnmmm. It must have been hectic hey.

It sounds like, you know, a group thing. What do you people normally call it? Group sex or something. (Laughs in mockery of Malisa and calls out at a colleague) Warrant Officer.

Come quickly. You will not believe what is going on here.

LIGHTS OUT

MOVEMENT SIX

Ongoing discussion.

MADALA: She is still not talking, Gogo. Not a single blink.

GOGO: Who would?

MADALA: The damage is deep.

GOGO: That is the only explanation to this deafening silence.

MADALA: The damage is deep. What can one say? Not many options for the poor in this country. Justice has become expensive. Rape is committed with arrant impunity these days. Rich men who murder their lovers get nice trials and treated like celebrities, even inside jails.

GOGO: Let my ancestors not sleep, otherwise let my life become miserable and let my grand-child live *(Sobs)*. Dear ancestors. Do not be quiet on me now. My life is ebbing away before my

26

eyes. I am dying. Can you not see?

MADALA: Be strong, Gogo. This family needs you alive.

GOGO: What is the essence of life if it is lived in misery?

No point! How could I be alive and witness my child loose her mind? What is the point of living?

LIGHTS OUT

MOVEMENT SEVEN

Police Station (Continuing.)

SERGEANT MALINGO:

> You have refused to even say a word. Ok. (He writes) Victims were tied up. And then raped. So, tell me. Did you at least enjoy it? Did you em... em... come? I am sure you know what is meant by to come. You see, I am just doing my job here. So, here is the question again. Did you, em... em... come? As in...

MALISA: *(She speaks inaudibly.)*

SERGEANT MALINGO:

> Say that again.

MALISA: *(Speaks very quietly.)*

SERGEANT MALINGO:

> I did not hear you. Again please. You see, I must write something. It will assist investigations. You understand?

MALISA: *(Beckons on Sargent Malingo to come closer. He does.)*

SERGEANT MALINGO:

Yes. I am here. So, did you?

Malisa again motions Sergeant Malingo to bend towards her. He does. She speaks very quietly into his ears.

SERGEANT MALINGO:

(Surprised/embarrassed) Excuse me?

Malisa motions Sergeant Malingo to bend closer still. He does. She bites his hear off. He screams. Officers in the Police station storm out with guns drawn. As she is taken away, she spits the bitten-off part of the hear on Sargent Malingo who kneels, holding on to his chopped off ear, screaming in pain.

LIGHTS OUT

MOVEMENT EIGHT

Gogo sits, dejected. Madala enters, half drunk.

GOGO: How is my child?

MADALA: Fast asleep. Nothing has changed. She was granted bail.

GOGO: Her mother blames me. She is still not talking to me.

My grandchild is devastated.

MADALA: She has refused to eat still. How many days now?

GOGO: Two.

MADALA: She is in shock and traumatised.

GOGO: Who would not be?

MADALA: The Police officer lost an ear.

GOGO: Just an ear?

MADALA: Gogo?

GOGO: How could you ask a rape victim if she had orgasm during rape?

MADALA: Could it be true, though? Do you? Do you also have orgasm?

GOGO: That interrogation was beyond ridicule. Insensitive does not even explain it. Very disgusting. He got what he deserved.

MADALA: You approve of violence, Gogo?

GOGO: Not violence. It is corporal punishment. Some men deserve such. Even the death penalty.

MADALA: You approve of the death penalty Gogo?

GOGO: Of course I do.

MADALA: Gogo?

GOGO: Stop screaming. You have not received a death penalty. At least not yet.

MADALA: But you just wished me dead.

GOGO: Many times. Rapists and murderers keep increasing and the crime keeps escalating in our communities.

MADALA: *(In stupor)* Is it true?

GOGO: What about femicide?

MADALA: *(In stupor)* Femicide? I honestly do not know anything about that one. Is he in town?

GOGO: (Ignores him) Life has become very cheap today. The death penalty will reduce that scourge in a hurry.

MADALA: That officer lost an ear. Is that not enough punishment?

GOGO: He should have lost more. That interrogation was out of order.

MADALA: Gogo!

GOGO: In my days, men who raped lost more than ears. Some lost their things.

MADALA: (In stupor) What things?

GOGO: Idiot! Their major instrument of atrocity.

MADALA: (In stupor) You do not make sense.

GOGO: Fool! Their dicks.

Madala dozes off. Gogo, knife in hand, stealthily goes to Madala and unzips his trousers.

MADALA: (Wakes up) Gogo what are you about?

GOGO:	I wanted to show you the instrument, idiot.
MADALA:	Got you! You will never find it there. It is now in my pocket. Girls today are very dangerous so it must be kept safe. (zips his trousers) That is the idea.
GOGO:	I hate men.
MADALA:	Your father was a man.
GOGO:	Noble man. He was different. He worked at the mines and he lived an honest life. Your father met my mum after my father passed away.
MADALA:	Our mother was a gift.
GOGO:	She would kill you if she was here to hear the way you treat me.

Madala staggers to get a refill. He returns.

| MADALA: | *(Reflective)* You know what? I also want to be a noble man, even if it is in my dreams. Noble is noble. Whether real or imagined, just be |

noble. Tell me, you were saying that you hated men.

GOGO: I still do.

MADALA: No! Do not say that. Your pastor will excommunicate you.

GOGO: I hate my pastor too.

MADALA: You hate your pastor? Now I know that you are the Satan.

GOGO: I care less.

MADALA: Yes, just like Satan. Heartless!

GOGO: Although I was the victim, I used them very well to my advantage. I retired all the men who came to me. I used them. I wasted them. It was my own revenge. I twerked for them and fucked them because that was all they ever wanted. I also wasted them because that was all I needed to do.

MADALA: Gogo?

GOGO: I have been there and done all that. Girls today are too timid. In my days, we were well mannered when treated well by men, but vicious when humiliated.

MADALA: Some girls today could also be vicious.

GOGO: They are not.

MADALA: They are.

Malisa comes out of the room. and merely walks past them and out of the house.

GOGO: The appointment is for today.

MADALA: We can only hope she gets help and evidence for the Court. This whole thing might terrify her the more, Gogo. It was hell at the Police station.

GOGO: My child is dead already.

MADALA: Do not say that.

GOGO: Let us hope the hospital helps.

MADALA: You see, I was wondering. Maybe she and her friends were attacked and raped because they came out that they were lesbians. This is Africa Gogo.

	Not America. People should know.
GOGO:	That is not enough reason to be attacked and raped.

LIGHTS OUT

MOVEMENT NINE

Malisa is in a hospital, standing before a Doctor.

DOCTOR: *(Sits behind a desk, taking notes.)* 21 years. You are an adult. Sit down.

DOCTOR: I know it could be traumatic for an impressionable mind as yours. But what can we do? *(Points at the examination table.)* Lie down here and remove your underwear.

Malisa looks at him viciously. She removes her underwear.

DOCTOR: Ok. Spread your legs. *(He focuses the examination lights on an uninspired Malisa).* Open it wide for me. Perfect! *(He examines)* Oh! Not again! You see, you ought to have come here straight from the Police station. In fact, the Police were supposed, under the law, to bring you here. *(He examines some more and continues)* It has been two days. Now all signs of evidence are lost because you had a shower already. As you would imagine, every form of their DNA is lost. Well, the bruises are there but you see, more evidence is lacking. The Court will ridicule us again. They always do that to us, and to the victims who are in anguish. You can get up now. I will make a report. Let us hope we are lucky to get appropriate convictions and sentencing.

Malisa gets up and makes to leave. The Doctor points at the underwear on the floor but Melisa just looks at him and leaves. The Doctor picks it up and looks at it very closely under the lights.

DOCTOR: And there could be some evidence you know. You never know hey. DNAs could be crazy these days *(He smells it.)* Perfect!

LIGHTS OUT

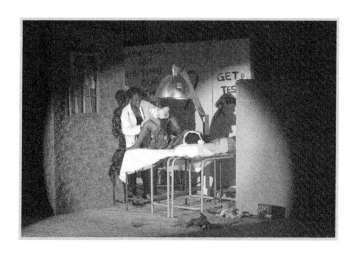

Malisa @ The Hospital

MOVEMENT TEN

The Court is in session in a tensed atmosphere. Up Centre Stage is the Judge, overlooking the defence counsel standing and cross examining the victim who is standing in the witness' stand. The six accused men stand adjacent.

DHLAMINI: Your honour, it is preposterous.

DIKKO: What?

JUDGE: What is preposterous, Counsel?

DHLAMINI: For the prosecuting counsel to even think, albeit suggest, that the victims seduced the accused persons.

JUDGE: The Counsel made no such accusation.

DIKKO: Did they twerk? Yes, they did.

JUDGE: *(To Dhlamini.)* Did they twerk?

DHLAMINI: Yes, your honour. That is what they do for the money. It is a job.

DIKKO: A little education will suffice here your honour.

JUDGE: This Court shall oblige.

DIKKO: A definition, your honour. Twerking is dancing to popular music in a sexually provocative manner involving thrusting hip, ass movements and a low, squatting stance *(a model comes out to demonstrate as Dikko speaks)*.

DHLAMINI: It is a job your honour.

DIKKO: No contest. A question, though.

JUDGE: Yes, you may.

DIKKO: Is this twerking, this job, is it seductive?

DHLAMINI: My lord?

JUDGE: What is your answer, Counsel?

DHLAMINI: My lord?

DIKKO: Counsel is grandstanding. Is this job seductive? That is the question.

DHLAMINI: My lord, this is....

DIKKO: Your honour, the counsel is going around in circles.

JUDGE: Let me be the judge of that.

DHLAMINI: This whole exercise has become but a joke.

JUDGE: Let the Counsel be wary of words uttered in this court.

DHLAMINI: This honourable court has been approached for a redress, my lord. The Court's tardiness is frustrating, to say the least, my lord. This could lead to impatience on the part of the victim. My lord, this court ought to expedite hearings and judgement on matters such as this, otherwise....

DIKKO: My lord, Counsel is suggesting the victim could take matters into her hands?

JUDGE: I did not observe that at all.

DIKKO: It was apparent enough in his submission, your honour. That is extrajudicial.

DHLAMINI: My lord.

DIKKO: Counsel suggests that victims take the law into their own hands.

JUDGE: Did he?

42

DHLAMINI: Counsel is beside himself, my lord.

DIKKO: He just blatantly declared war on our judiciary.

JUDGE: Let me be the judge of that.

DHLAMINI: My lord, my colleague's demeanour is a complete abuse of this judiciary process.

JUDGE: I shall be the judge of that.

DHLAMINI: This is a farce.

JUDGE: A farce?

DIKKO: My lord.

JUDGE: Quiet!

DHLAMINI: My lord.

JUDGE: And quiet, too! Listen, both of you. Your utterances beg contempt of my court and you might regret if they are not tamed. I shall dully make observations of inconsistencies, misunderstanding and possible contempt in your submissions, Counsels.

BOTH

COUNSELS: As the Court pleases.

DHLAMINI: Your honour, if due diligence is exercised in this matter, the accused are the monsters that need taming.

DIKKO: That is prejudicialis injurious, your honour. The Counsel is seducing this Court in favour of preconceived ideas. This could result in harm or injury to the accused.

JUDGE: Counsel must refrain from prejudicial insinuations.

DIKKO: Counsel is in contempt.

JUDGE: *(To Dhlamini)* Counsel?

DHLAMINI: Your honour, it is laughable for the prosecuting counsel to suggest that the victim seduced the accused. Besides, jurisdiction is a factor to be considered here.

JUDGE: Clarify your submission, Counsel.

DHLAMINI: The three victims were doing their job at the club. The incident occurred after hours.

DIKKO: Your honour, the accused paid to access the venue. It is routine. They paid for the services. It is the norm.

DHLAMINI: Objection, your honour!

JUDGE: Overruled! You may continue, Counsel.

DIKKO: The accused had the rights to receive all services at the club. They paid for their presence as well as conducts.

JUDGE: Any objection to that, Counsel?

DHLAMINI: Your honour, before this results into a circus, I must remind this honourable Court that the incident occurred after office hours, away from the club. How is that for paying for services at the club?

Suddenly, Malisa charges towards the six accused sitting on the opposite side of the courtroom. She is restrained by the police but she manages to retrieve a firearm from the Court Police and immediately holds the Court Police hostage.

MALISA: Here we go! This would go down one way or another. Peacefully or with a lot of casualties. Move only if you are ready to die.

DETECTIVE

BETHRAND: *(Draws a side firearm)* Drop that weapon or you will be wasted.

JUDGE: This is a court. You cannot possibly do that. Somebody must restrain this woman at once.

DETECTIVE

BETHRAND: You do not know how to use that thing.

MALISA: Watch me surprise you. *(Malisa shoots into the air)* That was not an accident.

JUDGE: *(Furiously to Dhlamini)* You may want to clarify to this Court the meaning of your client's assault on the court.

DETECTIVE

BETHRAND: Last warning. Drop that weapon or you are dead.

MALISA: Too late. I am already dead. I am
             a ghost. I died since the day I was
             raped. We died. Pull that trigger
             if you are a man with balls. Pull
             it!

DETECTIVE

BETHRAND: Do not try my patience. I will not
             hesitate.

MALISA: How old are you?

DETECTIVE

BETHRAND: *(Hesitates)* 35. Why?

MALISA: As a cop?

DETECTIVE

BETHRAND: 15.

MALISA: You became a police officer at the
             age of 20.

DETECTIVE

BETHRAND: Drop your weapon.

MALISA: Old enough to be a criminal,
             right?

DETECTIVE

BETHRAND: I will not hesitate.

MALISA: Are you different?

DETECTIVE

BETHRAND: Different?

MALISA: Pull that trigger if you have never raped a woman in your 35 miserable years on earth.

DETECTIVE

BETHRAND: *(Looks around the Court. Shamefully lowers his weapon)*

JUDGE: This Court will adjourn.

MALISA: *(To the Judge)* How old are you?

JUDGE: You cannot interrogate me. This is my Court.

MALISA: Not anymore. Have you ever raped a woman?

JUDGE: I am not under interrogation.

MADALA: Idiot. Answer the fucking question, bastard!

MALISA: *(To Madala)* Shut up old man. Normal human beings are having a conversation here.

MADALA: Malisa, it is I your Uncle. I am a normal human being.

MALISA: Oh! Really? Let us talk then. Speak.

MADALA: Speak what?

MALISA: How many times? Tell everyone here and now, Madala. How many times?

MADALA: What are you saying? How many times of what?

MALISA: How many times have you raped me? Yes, tell the world.

MADALA: Nonsense!

(Malisa shoots into the air)

MALISA: How many times?

MADALA: Just fifteen times.

(Malisa shoots Madala. Gogo faints. Everyone is petrified)

MALISA: *(To the Judge)* Now, shall we go over those lines again, Mr Judge?

JUDGE: *(To the Court police)* Get that woman.

MALISA: How old are you?

JUDGE: You cannot interrogate me. This is my court.

MALISA: Not anymore. Have you ever raped a woman?

JUDGE: I am not under interrogation.

Malisa shoots into the air.

MALISA: Will you speak or should I make you speak?

JUDGE: *(Petrified)* Yes. I mean no, your honour. I am 64 years old. It was a very long time ago your honour. She was actually my girlfriend, but that day I was very horny and she was not willing. So, I...

MALISA: You raped her!

JUDGE: Forgive me your honour. Like I said, she was my girlfriend and it is now a very long time ago, your honour. And in actual fact, I was...

MALISA: Quiet! The judiciary has become a charade. Your jokes end here today. A tree is known by its fruits. Your fruits as judiciary have become worrisome and pathetic. Women in this country have no defence from their men. Their lovers. Court clerk.

COURT

CLERK: *(Scared)* Yes, mayor. I mean yes, your honour.

MALISA: Check the records. How many rape cases in Courts this past year?

COURT

CLERK: *(Hurriedly checks the records)* More girls and women have been raped and murdered in the past year. 291 cases more than the penultimate year.

MALISA: Convictions?

COURT

CLERK: Not commensurate to offences.

MALISA: And why is that?

COURT

CLERK: Am not sure your honour. Most offenders were released on bail. Cases tend to evaporate after

several adjournments. Counsels
and victims get tired of Court
sittings.

MALISA: There have been meagre convictions of these heinous crimes in
recent times. Rapes everywhere,
every time. Men continue to
murder the women they swore to
protect, love and cherish. It is
already an epidemic. Is this it?

*Malisa's firearm goes off again. Presently, a TV crew
comes in for a live broadcast of the ongoing:*

MALISA: Is this the country we pledge to
build? Our communities are no
longer safe. Women and girls are
not safe from rape, femicide and
gender based violence. Children
are no longer safe from gang
violence and drugs. What have
we done to us? What have we
done to generations unborn? Is
this the rainbow nation we
want?

SOLO: Nkosi sikelel' iAfrika
               Maluphakanyisw' uphondo
               lwayo, (Lord bless Africa, May
               her glory be lifted high) Yizwa
               imithandazo yethu, Nkosi
               sikelela, thina lusapho lwayo.
               (Hear our prayers, Lord bless us,
               your children).

MALISA: Are our ancestors proud of us
               today? In sane societies, men
               protect their women. Ours have
               become lunatics, raping and
               killing girls and women with
               impunity. That is the joke that
               we have now become.

*Nandy and Nelly come in. They walk to the Judge's
table, takes off their tops and lie down on it. Malisa
shoots into the air several times. Throws the gun at
the Court Police. Walks up to the table where Nelly
and Nandy lie. Removes her top and speaks.*

MALISA: We call on you dogs all over. We
               are now on national television.
               Come over here, rapists. All men
               who maim, rape and murder
               little girls and women. Come. If

you are not cowards, come out now in this public space and do what you do best. Animals. Come. Bring your cocks. Come screw. Come fuck. Come screw little children, come fuck your sisters and mothers, and grandmothers. Come on cowards. Anyone of you out there?

SOLO: Morena boloka setjhaba sa heso, O fedise dintwa le matshwenyeho, O se boloke, O se boloke setjhaba sa heso, Setjhaba sa, South Afrika, South Afrika.

(Lord we ask you to protect our nation, Intervene and end all conflicts, protect us, protect our nation, the nation of South Africa, South Africa)

The six accused men make to move towards the three protesting women.

COURT

POLICE: Do not even think about it! One more step and you are all dead.

54

MALISA: *(To the Police officer)* Too late,
              hypocrite! Where was the police
              when we were raped? What
              makes you think you can protect
              us now? *(To the accused rapists)*
              Come. No one will stop you now.
              Come finish what you started.
              Come, animals. Fools. Vultures.
              Come.

The men move to where the women lay. Remove their
own clothes and cover the naked bodies of the women.

MALISA: But if you will not do it in the
              open, why then do you do it in
              the closet? Stop all this nonsense
              at once. Let us build a res-
              pectable world. We are not
              animals. Let us make our pro-
              genitors proud of our conducts
              today. May this become the most
              noble vocation of men around
              our world.

Malisa hands herself to the Court Police. All freeze on
stage. While the news anchor reports, the Court
police leads Malisa out, with Nandy and Nelly in
tow.

News Report

You are live on Southern Agency Television. The hostage situation at the Magistrate Court is now over and the accused hostage taker, a certain Malisa who is a final year student at the University has been taken into custody, although no charges has been laid on her as yet.

Patricia Baloyi,

Southern Agency Television

GLOSSARY

MADALA: An elderly Uncle in a South African language

GOGO: A grandmother in South African language

The Court Scene

Malisa's Hostage Taking

Malisa's Arrest After Hostage Situation

For comments or feedback:
Email: *olakriso@yahoo.com*
Facebook: *Ola Kris Akinola*

Printed in Great Britain
by Amazon

78242906R00037